YOU VOTED
TOP TEN DU

10. What do you get when you place a dozen dumb blondes in a freezer? *See page 1*
9. What's a dumb blonde's favorite Christmas carol? *See page 8*
8. What does an intelligent blonde have in common with Big Foot? *See page 1*
7. How do you drown a dumb blonde? *See page 3*
6. What's a dumb blonde's idea of safe sex? *See page 25*
5. What do dumb blondes do for the environment? *See page 53*
4. How is a dumb blonde like a beer bottle? *See page 1*
3. What do you call five dumb blondes sitting in a circle? *See page 23*
2. What can strike a dumb blonde without her knowing it? *See page 6*
1. Which children's story is a dumb blondes favorite? *See page 1*

PLUS 270 HILARIOUS OTHERS!

"Outrageously funny."
- *Laughing Matters*

"Blondes are the latest scapegoats in the world of jokes... (which arc) speeding crazily around the country..."
- *Allure*

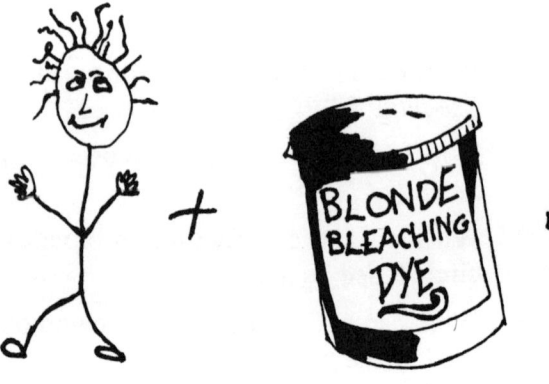

The Ultimate Dumb Blonde Joke Book

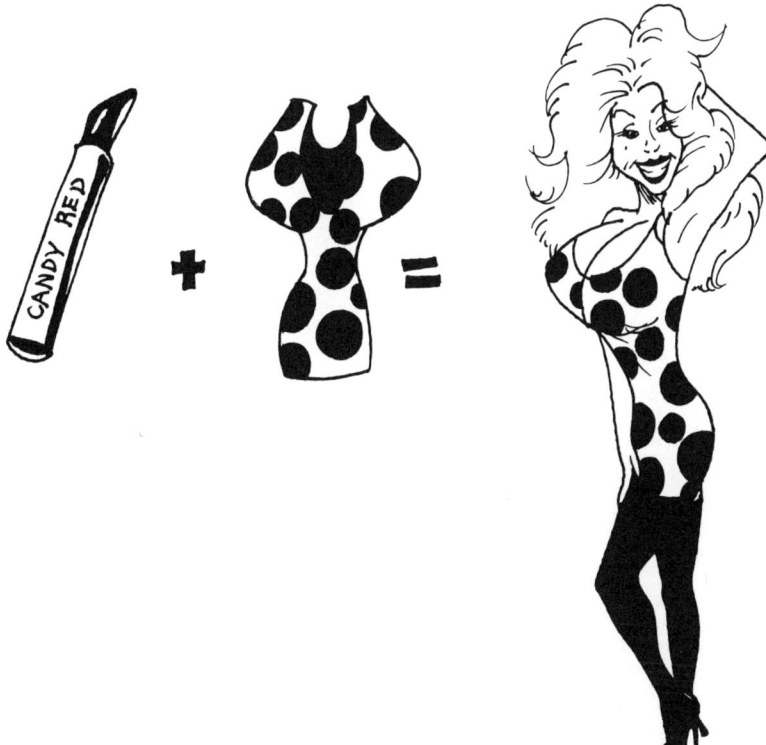

The Ultimate Dumb Blonde Joke Book

EVA RAE STUART

Illustrations by Todd Schowalter
Spot Art by Megan O'Neill

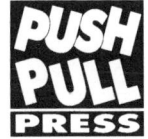

Thanks are due the following: Jerry Jenkins for his support and inspiration, Joseph S. Ajlouny for his efforts in getting it published, and dozens of friends from near and far for their excellent contributions, especially Lisa A. McDonald, Robert N. Alexander, and Debra S. Massoud.

Copyright © 1992 by JSA Publications, Inc.
All rights reserved.

The disclaimer at the end of this book
shall constitute a continuation of this notice.

Published by Push/Pull/Press,
an imprint of JSA Publications, Inc.
P.O. Box 37175, Oak Park, MI 48237

Printed in the United States of America
2 3 4 5 6 7 8 9 0

ISBN: 0-929957-05-9
Library of Congress Catalog Number: 92-80467

Additional copies of this and other Push/Pull/Press
humor books are available by calling toll free
1-800-345-0096

*To all the intelligent blondes of the world
—of whom I presumptuously include myself.
We know how to take a joke, don't we?*

1

What's a dumb blonde's favorite nursery rhyme?
Hump-me, Dump-me.

* * *

What do you get when you put ten dumb blondes in a freezer?
Frosted flakes.

* * *

Why is a dumb blonde like a beer bottle?
They're both empty from the neck up.

* * *

What did the dumb blonde say when asked if she'd ever been picked up by "the fuzz"?
"No, but I've been swung around by the tits."

* * *

What do an intelligent dumb blonde and Big Foot have in common?
Nobody has seen either one.

* * *

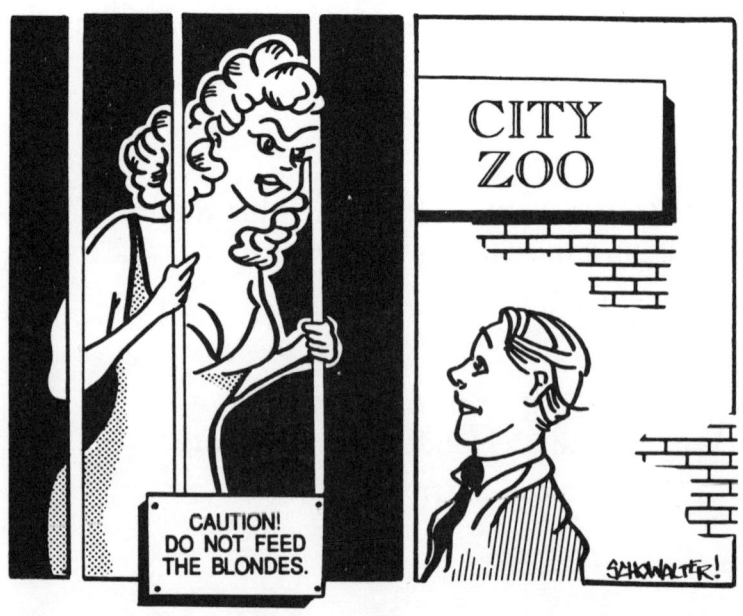

What is the best place to take a dumb blonde with PMS on a date?

* * *

How do you make a blonde drown?
Install a mirror at the bottom of the swimming pool.

* * *

Why don't dumb blondes like to make Kool-Aid?
They can't fit 8 quarts of water in that little package.

* * *

What does a dumb blonde say when you blow in her ear?
Thanks for the refill.

* * *

What do you call a blonde behind the steering wheel of an automobile?
An air bag.

* * *

What's the difference between a blonde and a carpenter?
A blonde has longer nails.

* * *

What's the difference between a dumb blonde and your job?
Your job still sucks after six months.

* * *

What's the difference between dating a dumb blonde and travelling on the Starship Enterprise?
The Starship Enterprise goes where no man has gone before.

* * *

How is a dumb blonde like spaghetti?
They both squirm when you eat them.

* * *

What do you say to a dumb blonde with no arms and no legs?
"Nice tits!"

* * *

Why do dumb blondes wear shoulder pads?
(Move head from side to side and say in airheadese)
"Gosh, I don't know."

* * *

What is the mating call of a dumb blonde?
"Gee, I think I'm drunk."

* * *

Why does a dumb blonde take care when she turns off her alarm clock?
So she doesn't smudge her makeup.

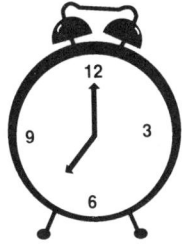

What can strike a dumb blonde without her knowing it?
A thought.

* * *

Why do dumb blondes go to R-rated movies in groups of 19 or more?
Because only over 18 are admitted.

* * *

Why do dumb blondes have T.G.I.F. on the tops of their shoes?
So they know Toes Go In First.

* * *

Why can't dumb blondes drive?
Because once they get in the front seat, they don't know what to do.

* * *

Why do dumb blondes use hair spray and mousse?
To catch what goes over their heads.

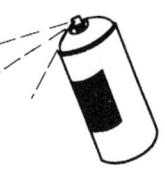

Why do you cover a dumb blonde's left ear when you blow in her right ear?
So she doesn't whistle.

* * *

What's the difference between a dumb blonde and a bottle of mineral water?
Mineral water contains no artificial coloring.

* * *

Why doesn't a dumb blonde snort coke?
Because the bubbles tickle her nose.

* * *

What's a dumb blonde's favorite Christmas song?
O Come All Ye Faithful.

* * *

What does a dumb blonde and a bowling ball have in common?
You can pick them up, throw them in the gutter, and they still come back to you.

How does a dumb blonde carry out a pregnancy test?
"Did you come inside me?"

* * *

How are dumb blondes and screen doors similar?
The more you bang them, the looser they get.

* * *

Why did the dumb blonde climb over the glass wall?
To see what was on the other side.

* * *

Why did the dumb blonde cross the road?
Never mind that, what was she doing out of the bedroom?

* * *

Why does a dumb blonde only change her baby's diaper every month?
Because it says on the box "good for up to 20 pounds."

* * *

Why did the dumb blonde get on the roof?
She heard that drinks were on the house.

* * *

What's the difference between a dumb blonde and an owl?
An owl says "who, who?", a dumb blonde says "whaaaat, whaaat?"

* * *

Why do dumb blondes like BMW's?
Because they can spell it.

* * *

Why do dumb blondes have more fun?
Because they don't know any better.

* * *

Why don't dumb blondes have elevator jobs?
They don't know the route.

* * *

What's a dumb blonde's favorite rock group?
Air Supply.

* * *

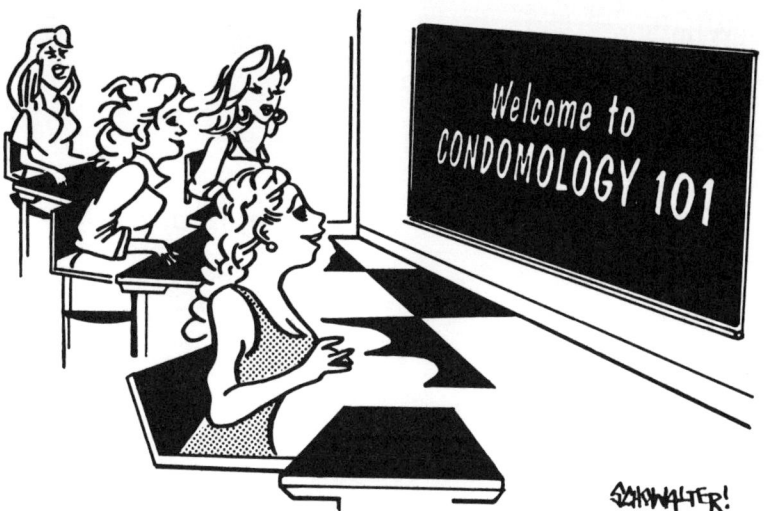

What is the number one college elective course for dumb blondes?

* * *

What's a blonde's favorite wine?
"Daaaddy, I want to go to Miaaami!"

* * *

What do you see when you look into a dumb blonde's eyes?
A vacancy sign.

What's the advantage of being married to a blonde?
You can park in the handicapped zone.

* * *

What does a dumb blonde call brown hair dye?
Artificial intelligence.

* * *

What is it called when a dumb blonde blows in another dumb blonde's ear?
A data transfer.

* * *

What's a dumb blonde's favorite cigarette?
More Longs.

* * *

What did the dumb blonde say when she found out she was pregnant?
"I hope it's not mine."

* * *

What did the dumb blonde call her pet zebra?
Spot.

* * *

What do you call a brunette between two dumb blondes?
An interpreter.

* * *

What do you call a dumb blonde between two brunettes?
A mental block.

* * *

How does a dumb blonde like her eggs on Monday?
Unfertilized.

* * *

According to a dumb blonde, how many seconds are there in a year?
Twelve. January second, February second. . .

* * *

How did the dumb blonde try to kill the bird?
She threw it off a cliff.

* * *

How do you get a dumb blonde to marry you?
Tell her she's pregnant.

* * *

How does a dumb blonde high-five?
She smacks herself on the forehead.

* * *

How do you make a dumb blonde laugh on Monday?
Tell her a joke on Friday.

* * *

How do you describe a dumb blonde, surrounded by drooling idiots?
Flattered.

* * *

What's the difference between a dumb blonde and a toothbrush?
You don't let your best friend borrow your toothbrush.

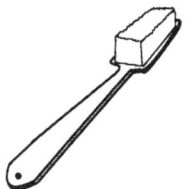

What did the dumb blonde jogger say after jogging around the world?
"Hi honey, I'm home."

* * *

What do you call a dumb blonde skeleton in the closet?
Last year's hide-and-seek champ.

* * *

What do you call a fly buzzing inside a dumb blonde's head?
A space invader.

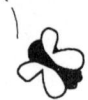

What do you call a dumb blonde in a tree with a briefcase?
A branch manager.

* * *

What did the dumb blonde say when she looked into a box of Cheerios?
"Oh look! Doughnut seeds!"

* * *

How do dumb blonde brain cells die?
Alone.

* * *

Why did the dumb blonde give her fiance wool socks?
She didn't want him to get cold feet.

* * *

How does a dumb blonde spell farm?
E-I-E-I-O.

* * *

How did the dumb blondes freeze to death?
They went to the drive-in movie to see "Closed For The Winter."

* * *

Why did the dumb blonde fill her water bed with beer?
Because she wanted a foam mattress.

* * *

How does a dumb blonde lose five pounds?
She takes off her make-up.

* * *

What does a dumb blonde call the time between her classes?
Inter-course.

* * *

Why does a dumb blonde go to a gynecologist?
To get a 2,000 men checkup.

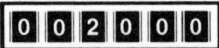

Why did it take the dumb blonde three tries to get pregnant?
She blew the first two.

* * *

How does a dumb blonde count money?
One, another one, another one. . .

* * *

Why do dumb blondes have orgasms?
So they know when to stop having sex.

* * *

Why aren't there many dumb blonde gymnasts?
Because when they do the splits, they stick to the floor.

* * *

How do you make a dumb blonde guy masterbate?

Put him in a jail cell with two black guys.

* * *

What job function would a dumb blonde have in an M & M factory?

Proofreading.

* * *

How many dumb blondes does it take to make chocolate chip cookies?

Thirteen—one to mix the batter and 12 to peel the M & M's.

* * *

Why did the dumb blonde dip her finger into her glass?

To see if it was a soft drink.

* * *

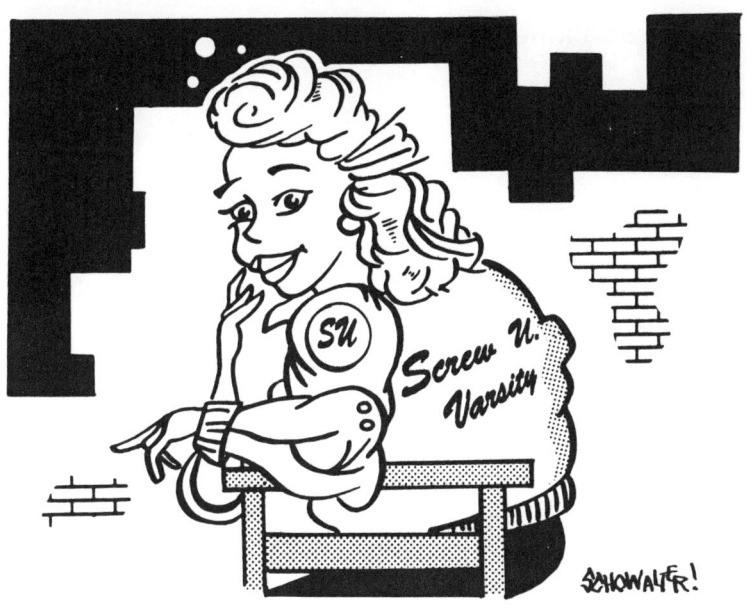

What college letter jacket do dumb blondes prefer to wear?

* * *

Why do blondes wear green lipstick?
Red means stop.

Why don't dumb blondes like bananas?
They can't find the zipper.

* * *

Why don't dumb blondes eat pickles?
They can't get their head in the jar.

* * *

Why do dumb blondes wear hoop earrings?
They have to have some place to rest their ankles.

* * *

Why do dumb blondes drive cars with sunroofs?
They offer more leg room.

* * *

Why did the dumb blonde fail at being a prostitute?
Because she gave blow-jobs for free.

* * *

Why can't dumb blondes in San Francisco wear miniskirts?
Because their balls will show.

* * *

What do you call ten dumb blondes sitting in a circle?
A dope ring.

* * *

What do you call ten dumb blondes lying down next to each other?
An air mattress.

* * *

What do you call ten dumb blondes with PMS and six dumb blondes with a yeast infection?
A whine and cheese party.

* * *

What do you call ten dumb blondes in a swimming pool?
Air bubbles.

* * *

What do you call ten dumb blondes in a basement?
A whine cellar.

* * *

What do you call ten dumb blondes sitting in a row?
An air line.

* * *

What do you call a dumb blonde with 150 IQ?
A golden retriever.

* * *

What does a dumb blonde call safe sex?
A padded dash board.

* * *

Why do dumb blondes have legs?
To get between the bedroom and the kitchen.

* * *

Why did the dumb blonde give up aerobics?
She couldn't keep her legs together long enough.

* * *

Why did the dumb blonde go halfway to Norway and then turn around and come home?
It took her that long to discover that a 14 inch Viking was a television.

Why do dumb blondes die before help arrives?
They always forget the 11 in 9-1-1.

* * *

Why do dumb blondes like tilt steering?
There's more headroom for maneuvering.

* * *

Why do dumb blondes wear patent leather shoes?
To check if their panties are still on.

Why are dumb blondes like corn flakes?
Because they're simple, easy, and they taste okay.

* * *

Why did God create dumb blondes?
Because dogs can't bring beer from the fridge.

* * *

Why do dumb blondes wear underwear?
To keep their ankles warm.

* * *

Why do dumb blondes have trouble achieving orgasm?
Who cares?

* * *

Why did the dumb blonde stop using the pill?
Because it kept falling out.

* * *

Why did the dumb blonde have a sore navel?
Because her boyfriend was also a dumb blonde.

* * *

Why do dumb blondes wash their hair in the kitchen sink?
That's where you wash vegetables.

* * *

Why did the deaf dumb blonde sit on a newspaper?
So she could lip read.

* * *

Why do dumb blondes have two more brain cells than a cow?
So they don't shit everywhere when you pull their tits.

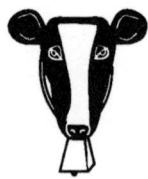

Why don't dumb blondes breast feed?
Because they always burn their nipples.

* * *

Why do dumb blondes work 7 days a week?
So you don't have to retrain them on Monday.

* * *

Why do dumb blondes take the pill?
So they know what day of the week it is.

* * *

What's the difference between a dumb blonde and a condom?

You only use a condom once.

* * *

What does a dumb blonde use for protection during sex?

A bus stop shelter.

* * *

What's the difference between dating a dumb blonde and fishing in Lake Erie?

You're less likely to catch something nasty in Lake Erie.

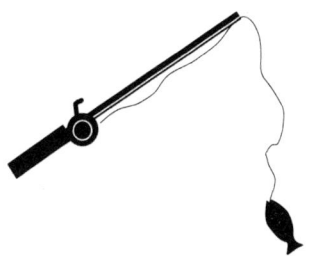

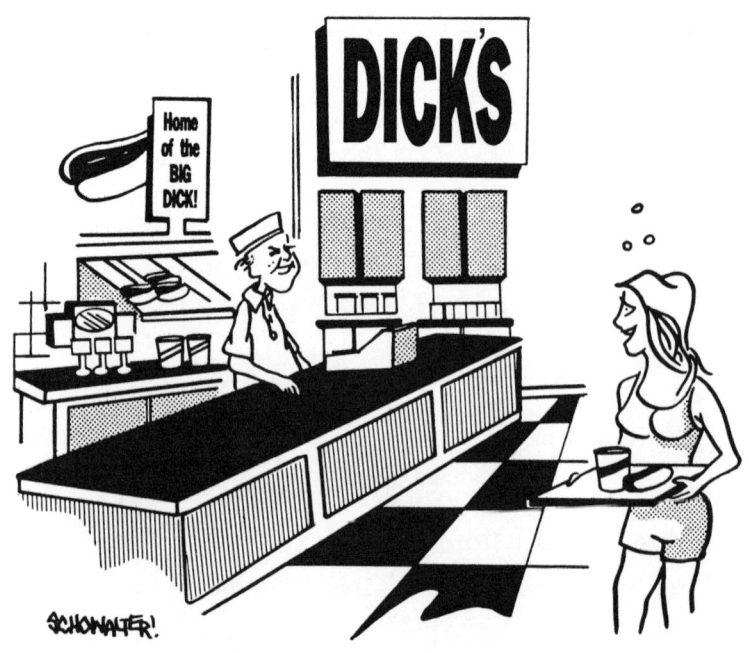

What do you call a dumb blonde's favorite hot dog stand?

* * *

Why did the dumb blonde join Greenpeace?
Because she heard they protect sperm whales.

* * *

What's the difference between a dumb blonde and Moby Dick?
A dumb blonde has swallowed more seamen.

* * *

What's the first thing a dumb blonde does in the morning?
She introduces herself.

* * *

What's the second thing a dumb blonde does in the morning?
She goes home.

* * *

Why do dumb blondes hate Santa Claus?
Because he only comes once a year.

* * *

What did the dumb blonde's mom say to her before the dumb blonde's date?

"If you're not in bed by midnight, come home."

* * *

What do you call a brunette hooker and three dumb blonde hookers?

Regular price, four bucks, four bucks, four bucks.

* * *

What does a computer and a dumb blonde have in common?

You don't appreciate either one of them until they go down on you.

* * *

What's the difference between a dumb blonde and a computer?

You only have to punch information into a computer once.

* * *

What did the dumb blonde think of the new computer?
She didn't like it because she couldn't get channel 9.

* * *

Why couldn't the dumb blonde terrorist blow up a car?
He kept burning his lips on the exhaust pipe.

* * *

What do you do when a dumb blonde throws a grenade at you?
Pull the pin out and throw it back.

* * *

What's the difference between a dumb blonde convention and Mars?
There could be intelligent life on Mars.

* * *

What's the worst thing about sex with a dumb blonde?

Bucket seats.

* * *

How does a dumb blonde turn on the lights after sex?

She opens the car door.

* * *

What do you say to a dumb blonde that won't give in?

"Have another beer."

* * *

What important question does a dumb blonde ask his/her mate before having sex?

"Do you want this by the hour, or the flat rate?"

* * *

What's brown, black and blue?

A brunette who's told too many dumb blonde jokes.

* * *

What do dumb blondes and cow pies have in common?
The older they get, the easier they are to pick up.

* * *

What do dumb blondes consider foreplay?
Removing their underwear.

* * *

What's the difference between a brick and a dumb blonde?
You can lay both, but a brick won't irritate you afterward.

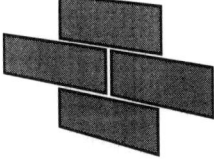

What does a dumb blonde like to see come out of a penis?
The wrinkles.

* * *

What's the difference between a dumb blonde and Snow White?

Snow White never slept with more than seven men at once.

* * *

How does a dumb blonde get rid of unwanted pubic hair?

Spits it out.

* * *

What do dumb blondes eat to increase their bust size?

Silicone chips.

* * *

Why did the dumb blonde have rectangular boobs?

She forgot to take the tissue out of the box.

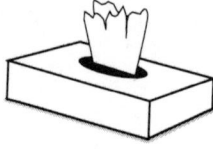

What do dumb blondes do with their assholes in the morning?
Pack them their lunch and send them to work.

* * *

What's the difference between a dumb blonde and a Porsche?
You don't lend out your Porsche to your friends.

* * *

What's the difference between a dumb blonde and a Delorean sportscar?
A Delorean is more difficult to get into.

* * *

What's the difference between a dumb blonde and a trampoline?
You take your shoes off before you get on a trampoline.

* * *

What does a dumb blonde guy call his girlfriend, a channel changer and a bag of chips?
"A threesome."

* * *

What's the difference between a dumb blonde track team and a tribe of sly pygmies?
One is a bunch of cunning runts, the other's a bunch of running cunts.

* * *

What's the difference between a dumb blonde aerobics class and a circus?
One is a group of cunning stunts, the other's a group of stunning cunts.

* * *

What's the difference between picking up a dumb blonde and a Cancun vacation?
There's only a 99 percent chance of sex on a Cancun vacation.

* * *

What's the difference between Gorbachev and a dumb blonde?
Gorbachev remembers the names of the seven guys who screwed him while on vacation.

* * *

What's the difference between a dumb blonde and the Panama Canal?
One is a busy ditch, the other's a dizzy bitch.

* * *

What's the difference between a skinny dumb blonde and a counterfeit bill?
One's a phoney buck, the other's a boney fuck.

* * *

What's the difference between a dumb blonde and Omar Sharif?
Omar Sharif doesn't bleach his moustache.

* * *

What's the difference between a dumb blonde and Wayne Gretsky?

Wayne Gretsky has never scored more than four times in 60 minutes.

* * *

What's the difference between a dumb blonde and a parrot?

You can teach a parrot how to say "No!"

What's black and fuzzy and hangs from the ceiling?

A dumb blonde electrician.

* * *

What did the dumb blonde say about anal sex?

"Don't mess with my brain."

* * *

What do dumb blondes and turtles have in common?
If they are on their backs, they're screwed.

* * *

How do you brainwash a dumb blonde?
Give her a douche and shake her upside down.

* * *

How do you tell if a dumb blonde did your landscaping?
The bushes are darker than the rest of the yard.

* * *

How do you tell when a dumb blonde reaches orgasm?
She drops her nail file.

* * *

How does a dumb blonde interpret 6.9?
A 69 interrupted by a period.

* * *

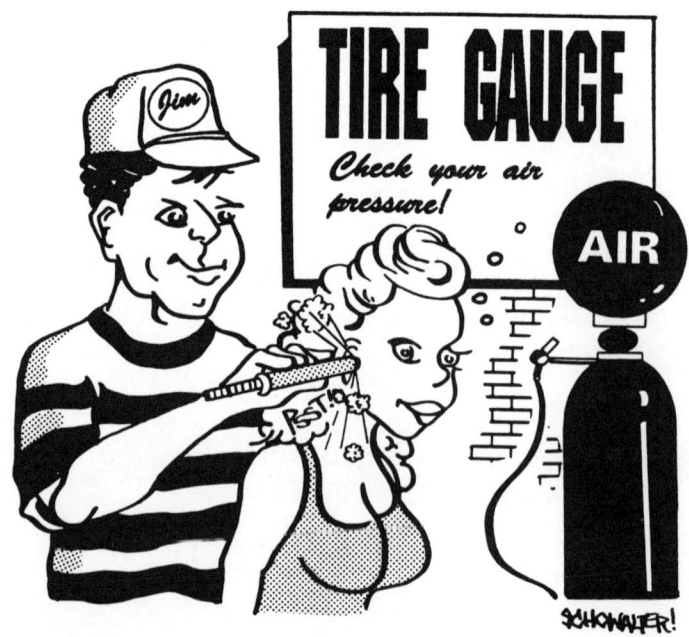

How do you measure a dumb blonde's IQ?

* * *

What does a dumb blonde answer to "are you sexually active?'
"No, I just lie there."

* * *

What's the difference between a dumb blonde girl and a dumb blonde guy?
The dumb blonde girl has a higher sperm count.

* * *

What's the difference between a dumb blonde having her period and a terrorist?
You can negotiate with a terrorist.

* * *

What do a 747 and a peroxide dumb blonde have in common?
They both have black boxes.

* * *

What do dumb blondes say after sex?
"So, are all you guys on the same team?"

* * *

What's the difference between a dumb blonde and the Titanic?

We know how many people went down on the Titanic.

* * *

What's the difference between a dumb blonde and a 747?

Not everyone has been on a 747.

* * *

What's the difference between a dumb blonde and Mt. Everest?

Only a few people have been up Mt. Everest.

* * *

What's the difference between butter and a dumb blonde?

Butter is more difficult to spread.

* * *

What's the difference between a dumb blonde and a telephone?

It costs 20 cents to use a telephone.

* * *

What's the difference between a dumb blonde's hairdo and a bottle of fabric softener?

Fabric softener contains no bleach.

* * *

Why did the dumb blonde get so excited after she finished her jigsaw puzzle in only six months?

Because on the box it said, "For 2–4 years."

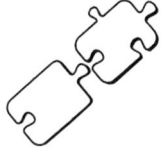

How many dumb blondes does it take to change a light bulb?

One. She holds it up in the socket and waits for the world to revolve around her.

* * *

What's the difference between a dumb blonde and a 5-watt light bulb?

A 5-watt bulb is brighter.

* * *

How can you tell if a dumb blonde is having a bad day?

Her tampon is behind her ear and she doesn't know what she's done with her pencil.

* * *

What does a dumb blonde say when asked to spell Mississippi?

"The state or the river?"

* * *

Did you hear about the dumb blonde that stayed up all night to see where the sun went?
It finally dawned on her.

* * *

Did you hear about the dumb blonde guy whose wife gave birth to twins?
He wanted to know who the other man was.

* * *

Two dumb blondes were observed in a parking lot trying to unlock the door of their Mercedes with a coat hanger.
Dumb blonde #1: I can't seem to get this door unlocked.
Dumb blonde #2: Well, you better hurry up and try harder, it's starting to rain and the top is down!

* * *

If you put a dollar on a dumb blonde's head, what do you get?
All you can eat for under a buck.

* * *

What do you call a zit on a dumb blonde's butt?
A brain tumor.

* * *

What did the dumb blonde do when she got her period?
Looked around for the person who shot her.

* * *

What type of guys do dumb blondes like?
The ones that give them the finger.

* * *

What do you give a dumb blonde before you start going out with her?
A complete medical.

What does a dumb blonde put behind her ears to make her more attractive?
Her ankles.

* * *

How do you make a dumb blonde's eyes sparkle?
Shine a flashlight in her ear.

On her way home the same dumb blonde drove past another sign that said "Clean Restrooms 8 Miles." By the time she drove eight miles, she had cleaned 43 restrooms.

* * *

Did you hear about the dumb blonde who committed suicide by swallowing peroxide?
She dyed by her own hand.

* * *

A policeman pulled a dumb blonde over after he/she's been driving the wrong way on a one-way street.
Cop: Do you know where you were going?
Dumb blonde: No, but it must have been a lousy party because everyone is leaving.

* * *

A dumb blonde and a brunette are walking down the street, the brunette says, "Look, a dead bird." The dumb blonde looks up and says, "Where?"

* * *

Two dumb blondes were walking along and came to some tracks, one dumb blonde said, "These look like deer tracks," and the other said, "No, they look like moose tracks." They were still arguing when the train hit them.

* * *

If a dumb blonde and a brunette both jumped off a building at the same time, who would land first?

The brunette. The dumb blonde would have to stop to ask directions.

* * *

Three dumb blondes are attempting to change a light bulb. One of them decides to call 911:
Dumb blonde: We need help. We're three dumb blondes changing a light bulb.
Operator: Hmmmmm. You put in a fresh bulb?
Dumb blonde: Of course.
Operator: And the switch is on?
Dumb blonde: Yes, yes.
Operator: And the bulb still won't light up?
Dumb blonde: No, it's working fine.
Operator: Then what's the problem?
Dumb blonde: We got dizzy spinning the ladder around and we all fell and hurt ourselves.

* * *

A dumb blonde was driving down the highway to Disneyland when she saw a sign that said "Disneyland Left." After thinking for a minute, she said to herself, "Oh, well," and turned around and drove home.

Disneyland LEFT

A pregnant dumb blonde, brunette and redhead were sitting in the gynecologist's office. The redhead commented, "I'm going to have a boy."
"How do you know?" asked the brunette.
"Because when my husband and I were making love, I was on top."
"That means I'm going to have a girl," responded the brunette, "because when we were making love, I was on the bottom."
The dumb blonde started to cry. "What's wrong?" asked the others. The dumb blonde weeped, "I'm going to have puppies!"

* * *

What do you see when looking into a dumb blonde's eyes?
The back of her head.

* * *

What did the father say to his dumb blonde daughter?
"Hard to believe you outswam all those other sperms."

* * *

What's a dumb blonde's idea of romance?
A lift home afterwards.

* * *

Why do dumb blondes go out in pairs?
So they have someone to keep score.

* * *

What do dumb blondes do for the environment?
They buy unleaded eyebrow pencils.

* * *

A dumb blonde locked his keys in his car. It took him over an hour to get his wife out.

* * *

Why do dumb blondes have TGIF on their shirts?
Tits Go In Front.

* * *

What does a dumb blonde say after multiple orgasms?
"Yea, team!"

* * *

The dumb blonde and her boyfriend were sitting in a hot tub when the dumb blonde said to her boyfriend, "Is it true that if you pull your finger out, I'll sink?"

* * *

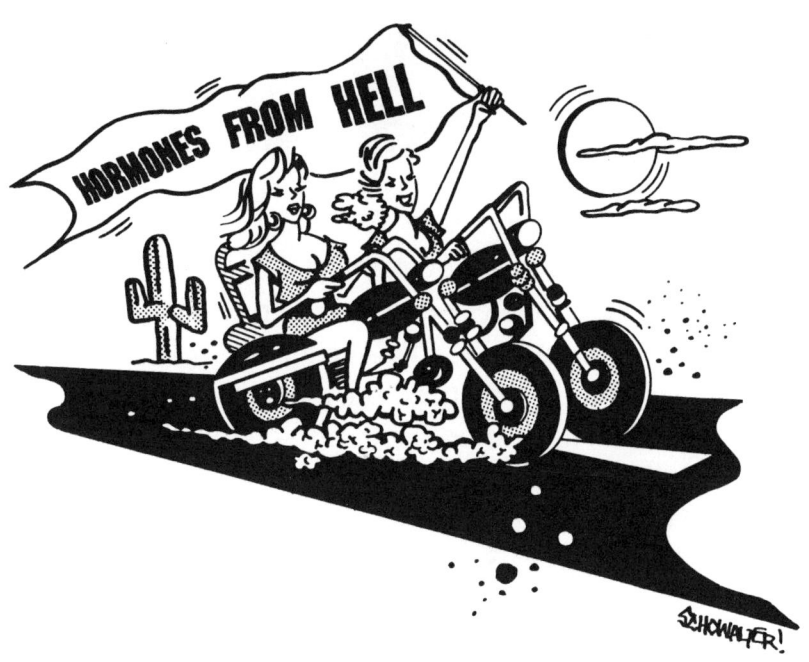

What do you call a dumb blonde motorcycle gang?

* * *

Did you hear about the dumb blonde who bought snow tires?
He stored them in his freezer.

* * *

A dumb blonde, a brunette and a redhead walk into a bar. The redhead walks up to the bartender and says, "I'd like an SS."
What's that?" questions the bartender.
"A scotch and soda," replies the redhead.
The brunette walks up to the bartender and asks for a WW.
"What's that?" questions the bartender.
"A whiskey and water."
The dumb blonde walks up to the bartender and asks for a 15.
"What's that?" questions the bartender.
"A seven and seven," replies the dumb blonde.

* * *

There were three people stranded on an island: a brunette, a redhead, and a dumb blonde. The brunette looked over the water to the mainland and estimated about 20 miles to shore. So she announced, "I'm going to try to swim to shore." So she swam out five miles, and got really tired. She swam out ten miles from the island, and she was too tired to go on, so she drowned.

The second one, the redhead, said to herself, "I wonder if she made it. I guess it's better to try to get to the mainland than stay here and starve." So she attempted to swim out. The redhead had a lot more endurance than the brunette, as she swam out 10 miles before she even got tired. After 15 miles, she was too tired to go on, so she drowned.

So the dumb blonde thought to herself, "I wonder if they made it! I think I'd better try to make it too." So she swam out 5 miles, ten miles, 15 miles, nineteen miles from the island. The shore was just in sight, but she said, "I'm too tired to go on!" So she swam back.

* * *

What do you say to a blonde who is too young for sex?

"Coochie-coochie-coo."

* * *

What does a dumb blonde do with guys who crash her parties?

She throws them out in the morning.

* * *

What's the difference between a dumb blonde and a visit to the doctor's office?

She doesn't say "Ahh" before opening her mouth.

* * *

What's a dumb blonde's idea of hard work?

Unbuttoning a man's fly.

* * *

What does a dumb blonde call a guy who reads Hustler?
An intellectual.

* * *

What do you give a dumb blonde after you've been going out with her for two weeks?
An eternity ring.

What's a dumb blonde's favorite book?
Once Is Not Enough.

* * *

What's a dumb blonde's favorite meal?
A hotdog and two brussel sprouts.

* * *

Why are most surfers blonde guys?
Because they're too dumb to get jobs.

* * *

What's the difference between a dumb blonde and a nickel sucker?
It costs five cents to lick a sucker.

* * *

What's a dumb blonde's favorite wine?
"I wanna 'nother Fuzzy Navel."

* * *

What are a dumb blonde's favorite drinks?
Sex on the Beach and Orgasms.

What's the difference between a dumb blonde and a fast food restaurant?

You can't get crabs in a fast food restaurant.

* * *

Why did the dumb blonde join a dating service?

Because she figured it was cheaper than arranging dates herself.

* * *

What's a dumb blonde's idea of sophistication?

Khalua flavored condoms.

* * *

Why did the dumb blonde complain about sexual harassment in the office?

Because the boss asked her to get down to some hard work.

* * *

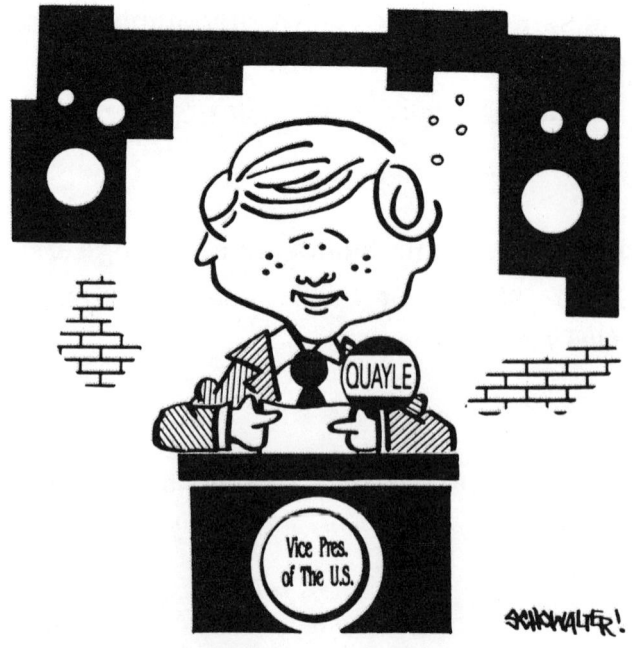

What do you call a dumb blonde that is accidentally born male?

* * *

What do you call a group of dumb blondes on rollerskates?

A mobile sperm bank.

* * *

What happened to the dumb blonde who bought a vibrator?

She knocked all her teeth out.

* * *

What's the best pick-up line to use on a dumb blonde?

"My Vette's outside, baby."

* * *

What does a dumb blonde say before sex?

"Hi, my name's Heather."

* * *

Why did the dumb blonde buy a bottle of Harvey's Bristol Cream?

Because she thought it was a new kind of massage lotion.

* * *

Why does a dumb blonde ask her man to keep his eyes shut during sex?

So he can't see her roots.

* * *

How do you offend a dumb blonde?

The answer to this question is still under study at NASA.

* * *

How does a dumb blonde prepare dinner for her guests?

"Hello, is this Meals on Wheels?"

* * *

What's the similarity between a dumb blonde and Lionel Richie?
They're both easy like Sunday morning.

* * *

Boyfriend asks a dumb blonde: "Fancy trying something from the Kama Sutra?"
"Nah, I don't like Indian food."

* * *

What's the difference between a dumb blonde and a master carpenter?
A dumb blonde has handled more tools.

* * *

What is a dumb blonde's idea of high class?
A silver dildo.

* * *

What's the difference between a dumb blonde's panties and a high class disco?
You have to pay to get into a disco.

* * *

What's a dumb blonde's favorite soft drink?
Seven Up.

* * *

What's the difference between a dumb blonde and a man imprisoned for life?
A dumb blonde has a higher sperm count.

* * *

What's the difference between a dumb blonde and hand-me-down clothes?
You know who's been inside the hand-me-downs.

* * *

What's the difference between a dumb blonde and a mirror?

You can't see through a mirror.

* * *

What's the difference between a dumb blonde and a condom?

You only use a condom once.

* * *

What's the difference between a dumb blonde and a caramel apple?

A caramel apple is more chewy and tastes great.

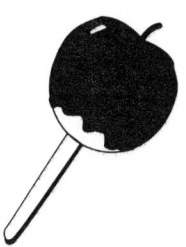

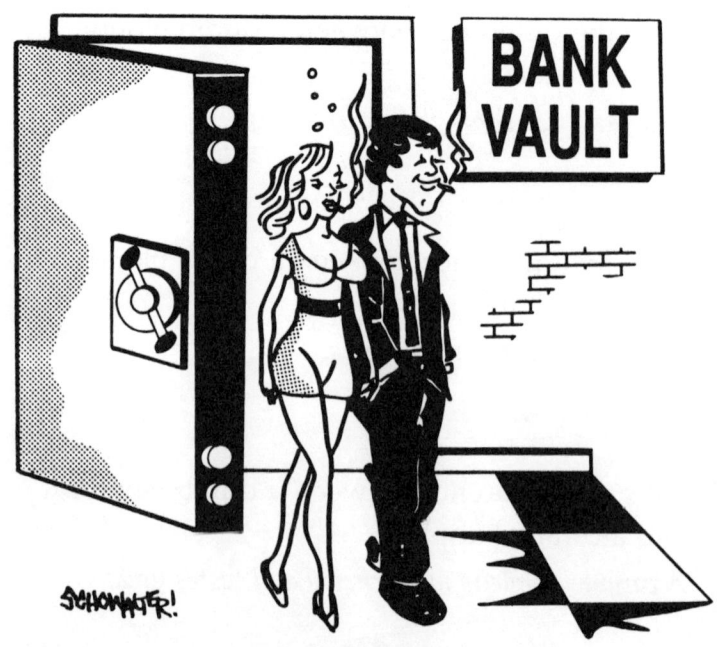

How do dumb blondes have safe sex?

* * *

What's the difference between a dumb blonde and a block of ice?
Not much.

* * *

What can you always conclude about a dumb blonde bodybuilder?
That he's got more muscle in his arms than in his brain.

* * *

What is the irritating part around a dumb blonde's vagina?
The dumb blonde herself.

* * *

What's the difference between a dumb blonde and Russian roulette?

With Russian roulette you've only got a one in six chance of being screwed.

* * *

What's the similarity between a dumb blonde and a vampire?

They both bite and suck at night.

* * *

What does a dumb blonde have in common with an electric light?

You can turn both on with a flick of a finger.

What's the best bet for a national dumb blonde holiday?
April Fools Day.

* * *

Why are dumb blonde jokes so short?
So brunettes can remember them.

* * *

Why are dumb blonde jokes so dumb?
So they can understand them.

* * *

Why are there so many dumb blonde jokes?
It gives brunettes something to do when they're home alone Friday nights.

* * *

What do you say to a dumb blonde who's got her act together?

"So, you're an individualist?"

* * *

What's a dumb blonde's idea of a confidential communication?

"Did you bring a condom?"

* * *

What do you call a dumb blonde who wears a plain black string bikini?

A conservative.

* * *

What did the interviewer tell the dumb blonde job applicant?
"You can put your clothes back on now, Miss."

* * *

What do you call dumb blondes who can't get picked up at a party?
Leftovers.

* * *

What's a dumb blonde's definition of a bad date?
A guy with a big wallet but a small cock.

* * *

What's a dumb blonde's definition of a pick-up bar?
Home away from home.

* * *

What does a dumb blonde have written on the back of her panties?

"Next"

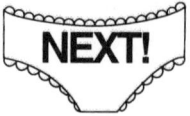

Why do redneck dumb blonde guys have two more brain cells than horses?

So they don't shit in the streets during parades.

* * *

How can you tell if a dumb blonde has been in your refrigerator?

By the lipstick on your cucumbers.

* * *

Why do dumb blondes wear red lipstick?

Because red means, "Stop, wrong hole."

* * *

What's the mating call of a brunette?
"Are you finished with the dumb blonde yet?"

* * *

What's the mating call of the horny, ugly dumb blonde?
(Screaming) "I said: I'm drunk!"

* * *

How is a dumb blonde guy's penis like a popsicle?
They both disappear after they've been sucked.

* * *

Why did the dumb blond keep touching the top of his head?
Because everyone said he was horny.

* * *

Why did the dumb blonde guy always wear a condom?
Because he was too lazy to take it off.

* * *

How do you change a dumb blonde's mind?
Blow in her ear.

* * *

How did the dumb blonde break her leg raking leaves?
She fell out of the tree.

* * *

What do you call a dumb blonde with half a brain?
Gifted.

* * *

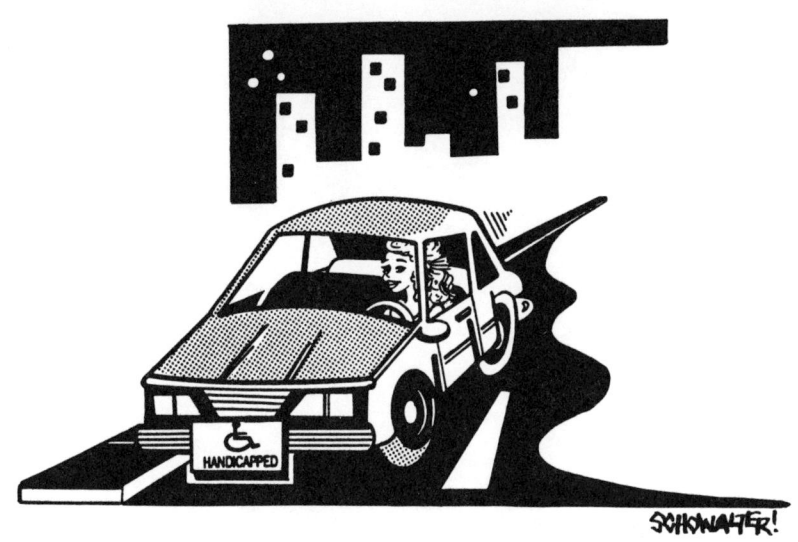

How do dumb blondes personalize their license plates?

* * *

Disclaimer of Copyright Notice

The author and publisher make no specific claim to the copyright of all the jokes contained herein, but have not knowingly violated the copyright of any person or entity in including them. The author and publisher assert their claim to all original jokes and other textual material, as well as to all art, drawings, and illustrations. This claim of copyright extends to the accumulation, conceptualization and presentation of this book.

For additional information please contact Push/Pull/Press at P.O. Box 37175, Oak Park, MI 48237 USA

Push/Pull/Press

ORDER FORM

Phone orders by credit card: (800) 345-0096

P.O. Box 37175
Oak Park, MI 48237
FAX (313) 546-3010

QTY	TITLE	UNIT COST	TOTAL
	The Ultimate Dumb Blonde Joke Book	$6.95	
	The Politically Incorrect Joke Book	$6.95	
	Gifts I Almost Got You	$7.95	
	The Book of Cold War Nostalgia	$9.95	
		Subtotal	
		Shipping & Handling	
		MI residents add 4% sales tax	
		TOTAL	

Yes, please send me the books indicated above. Add $1.25 shipping and handling for the first book and .50 for each additional book. Add $2.00 to total for books shipped to Canada. Overseas postage will be billed. Allow up to 4 weeks for delivery. Send check or money order payable to Push/Pull/Press. No cash or C.O.D.'s please. Quantity discounts available upon request.

SEND BOOKS TO:
NAME: _____

ADDRESS: _____

CITY _____ STATE ____ ZIP ____

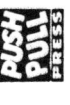

Push/Pull/Press

ORDER FORM

Phone orders by credit card: (800) 345-0096

P.O. Box 37175
Oak Park, MI 48237
FAX (313) 546-3010

QTY	TITLE	UNIT COST	TOTAL
	The Ultimate Dumb Blonde Joke Book	$6.95	
	The Politically Incorrect Joke Book	$6.95	
	Gifts I Almost Got You	$7.95	
	The Book of Cold War Nostalgia	$9.95	
		Subtotal	
		Shipping & Handling	
		MI residents add 4% sales tax	
		TOTAL	

Yes, please send me the books indicated above. Add $1.25 shipping and handling for the first book and .50 for each additional book. Add $2.00 to total for books shipped to Canada. Overseas postage will be billed. Allow up to 4 weeks for delivery. Send check or money order payable to Push/Pull/Press. No cash or C.O.D.'s please. Quantity discounts available upon request.

SEND BOOKS TO:
NAME:_____
ADDRESS:_____
CITY_____ STATE____ ZIP____

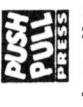

Push/Pull/Press

ORDER FORM

Phone orders by credit card: (800) 345-0096

P.O. Box 37175
Oak Park, MI 48237
FAX (313) 546-3010

QTY	TITLE	UNIT COST	TOTAL
	The Ultimate Dumb Blonde Joke Book	$6.95	
	The Politically Incorrect Joke Book	$6.95	
	Gifts I Almost Got You	$7.95	
	The Book of Cold War Nostalgia	$9.95	
		Subtotal	
		Shipping & Handling	
		MI residents add 4% sales tax	
		TOTAL	

Yes, please send me the books indicated above. Add $1.25 shipping and handling for the first book and .50 for each additional book. Add $2.00 to total for books shipped to Canada. Overseas postage will be billed. Allow up to 4 weeks for delivery. Send check or money order payable to Push/Pull/Press. No cash or C.O.D.'s please. Quantity discounts available upon request.

SEND BOOKS TO:
NAME: _____
ADDRESS: _____
CITY_____ STATE____ ZIP____